LETTERS TO A
CANCER PATIENT

LETTERS TO A CANCER PATIENT

Jennifer Lynne Opalewski

ELM HILL

A Division of
HarperCollins Christian Publishing

www.elmhillbooks.com

Published in Nashville, Tennessee, by Elm Hill, an imprint of Thomas Nelson. Elm Hill and Thomas Nelson are registered trademarks of HarperCollins Christian Publishing, Inc.

Elm Hill titles may be purchased in bulk for educational, business, fund-raising, or sales promotional use. For information, please e-mail SpecialMarkets@ThomasNelson.com.

All Scripture quotations are taken from the Holy Bible, New International Version®, NIV®. Copyright © 1973, 1978, 1984, 2011 by Biblica, Inc.® Used by permission of Zondervan. All rights reserved worldwide. www.Zondervan.com. The "NIV" and "New International Version" are trademarks registered in the United States Patent and Trademark Office by Biblica, Inc.®

Author photo credit Jayna Leigh Rumble

Library of Congress Cataloging-in-Publication Data

Library of Congress Control Number: 2018944794

ISBN 978-1-595557247 (Paperback)
ISBN 978-1-595557490 (eBook)

FOREWORD

At first the fevers were low grade and extremely intermittent. I caught a cold in October of 2015 that I could never seem to kick—even after rounds of antibiotics and steroids. I didn't think much of it at the time because I am a teacher and I normally get sick around October. In January, I started becoming very tired. By 7:00 PM, I would fall into bed after putting my daughter to bed and wake up feeling like I never got one minute of sleep. I attributed this to being back at work full-time and having a child to raise. In March 2016 my fevers intensified, and I developed a feeling that someone was constantly sitting on my chest. My doctor told me I needed Xanax—that I was just anxious—and the medicine would fix my problems. I never agreed with this because I knew my body and something was not right. In June, the fevers started coming every day and the simplest task (changing a diaper or walking downstairs) seemed to knock the breath right out of me. By July, I had a vein bulging out of my neck and my whole body felt swollen. Pressure had developed in my head that made opening my eyes a difficult task. I could no longer lie flat in my bed because it felt like my head was going to explode. In August 2016, I developed a pain in my arm so severe that I could barely move it. At this point, I had been to the doctor more than ten times. I was written off as a paranoid patient who they wanted to medicate with Xanax and send home. It was at this point that I decided to take myself to the hospital. My brother drove me and my Aunt Wanda met us there.

At twenty-eight years old, I found myself sitting in an emergency room bed with my aunt and younger brother as a first-year resident told me they found a mass in my chest and blood clots traveling up my left arm and into my neck. I was confused and scared. I felt sick. Something immediately began working its way from my stomach, to my chest, to my throat and then finally, out of my mouth came a heartbroken and pan-icked cry. I felt my soul shudder as I buried my face in my aunt's chest. Was I breath-ing? Was this a nightmare? Please, wake up. Please, wake up!

It wasn't a dream. It was my real life. I don't remember where the time went but now my mom was there. She was so frightened. One by one, my family mem-bers poured into my hospital room. The doctors admitted me immediately to the oncology floor, although they kept telling me they were not certain that it was can-cer. Two weeks in the hospital confirmed what the doctors expected. I had a type of non-Hodgkin's lymphoma. In other words, at twenty-eight years old I had cancer. I had the thing I feared more than anything. My life would never be the same. I thought I was too young to get cancer. How in this world could this happen to me? I'm healthy. I eat well. I don't drink too much. I've never smoked anything in my life. How could I do everything right but my body do me so wrong?

I wrote most of this book while undergoing chemotherapy but I am now one year post-chemo; however, it's still a daily battle—a fight I can't seem to win. I started writing about my experience as a form of therapy. I don't sleep well anymore. Most nights, I wake up in a panic hoping this isn't my life. In truth, it's taken me a long time to complete this book because whenever I sit down to write, I cry my eyes out. Will this ever get easier to talk about? I don't know. But to help me with my fight, my best friend Kayla had my family and friends each write me a letter based on an emotion I might be feeling. I open them when I am feeling that emotion and the letter is supposed to encourage me and lift my spirits. In many cases, these letters have pulled me out of difficult times. So, I wanted to write letters to fellow cancer patients with the hope that maybe one thing I share might help them with their own journey. At the very least, maybe this book will give them something to take their mind off things. I don't claim to be a doctor or therapist. I am just a twenty-eight-year-old girl whose life was turned upside down, and I am desperately trying to turn it rightside up.

DEDICATION

I dedicate this book to my daughter, Cecelia. If anyone wants to know what my heart looks like, all they have to do is look at you. May you always have the courage to chase your dreams but may you always remember that faith in Jesus and the love you show others is what defines your life and character. I love you so much!

To Larry, you are my true love and best friend. You are a pillar of strength and goodness. It's an honor to be your wife.

To my mom and dad, Donna and Joe, thank you for always believing in me. I love you both so much it makes my heart hurt. I admire both of you more than you will ever know.

To my sister, Jess, the first editor, the one who helped me realize my potential and the one who keeps me laughing. If there's an error, we know who to blame.

To my brother, Joey, thank you for taking me to the hospital and standing at my side as we heard the worst.

To my baby sister, Ally, thank you for stepping in and caring for my daughter when I couldn't. I love the way Cece loves you and I could never thank you enough for all you did and continue to do for us.

To Aunt Wanda, you're a true gift from above and you have the biggest heart. Thank you just doesn't seem like enough.

To my best friend, Kayla, you are the inspiration for all of this. Thank you for all you are and all you do.

To my family, they say it takes a village to raise a child. My life is a concrete example of that philosophy. I am so grateful I have had all of you as my village- through the ups and especially the downs, I have never once questioned your love and support. I would have liked to list you all by name, but it would be longer than this book. So, I will leave you with the words of our beloved Honey and Papa, "all my love, all my life- and that's the truth!"

CONTENTS

A Letter on Faith

"For God so loved the world that he gave his one and only Son, that whoever believes in him shall not perish but have eternal life."

JOHN 3:16

Ask yourself, do you believe that you have a purpose on this Earth? That your life is controlled and cared for by the Lord? Do you believe that He prepares you for what is coming your way?

I did not always answer yes to these questions. But they say hindsight is 20/20, right? Looking back on the events of my life, I realize that God was waiting for the perfect moment to give me cancer. No one escapes life without challenges, struggles, and adversity. It comes in all shapes and sizes. I never expected to have cancer. It wasn't in the plan I had for myself but thankfully, God had a better plan for me. We are reminded in the book of Jeremiah, *"For I know the plans I have for you,"* *declares the Lord, "plans to prosper you and* *not to harm you, plans to give you hope and* *a future"* (29:11). I didn't realize how the events of my life were preparing me for my battle with cancer but He knew. God was preparing my heart, my body, and my mind so I would come through without harm. He was breaking me down in so many areas of my life so I would be completely reliant on Him and I could prosper.

My life has been very easy. I have wonderful parents, my siblings and cousins are my best friends. My daughter is my whole world, and believe me when I say I

don't deserve my husband. I was raised in a
Maronite Catholic home and was privileged
enough to attend private school. I rarely
questioned things and lived my life bliss-
fully. My faith in the Lord began very early
in my life—but it was a faith based on fear
and struggling to do good deeds to secure
my spot in heaven. Regardless, I desired to
be close to the Lord and continued chasing
after Him and reading the gospel. The Lord
began placing people in my life who would
prove instrumental to the strengthening of
my faith.

I had a boyfriend in high school—whose
mother I feared—whose life I admired. His
faith was so steady and he was so confident
in his beliefs that I had to know more. I
began attending church with him and his
family; however, I would lie to my parents
about where I was going on Sunday morn-
ings—years later they would tell me they
knew exactly what I was doing. I was afraid
of the judgment of my family—my ethnic
Maronite Catholic family—who seemed

to watch every step I took. I didn't think I could handle their judgment. I tried to hide my enthusiasm for the Lord for as long as I could but it didn't last forever. My parents would question me and they were concerned I was going down the wrong road. When that boyfriend and I broke up our freshman year of college, I think my family thought that was the end of my interest in the Christian church—but it was just the beginning. As my dad says, "He was the best first boyfriend a father could ask for." I know why my dad says this but really this boyfriend is the reason I started to pursue the Lord, so he actually was the best first boyfriend.

This new interest in my faith led me to the absolute love my life—Larry, my now husband. We met through mutual friends in college and knew from the start we had a good thing. He quickly became the only boy I cared to know. His faith was strong and he was more steadfast than anyone I had ever met. In so many ways, he was incredibly attractive to me. We began attending church and grew together in our faith. It was after a few years of attending church that I decided to make a permanent decision to dedicate my life to the Lord.

Our church was doing a series called "Fail." The pastor was talking about life failing you. People shared heartbreaking stories but each person was able to share hopeful and positive outcomes because of their faith. I distinctly remember thinking life hasn't failed me yet but when it does, I want to know without question that I can rely on God. I believe this was God trying to deliberately move me towards Him because He knew what my future held.

I have had so many of these quiet, special moments where I've literally felt myself get closer to the Lord. My faith grows exponentially during these times. By the time I was given my cancer diagnosis, I had gone through breaking family traditions that in turn broke my mom's heart, I had suffered a bizarre infection upon returning from our honeymoon, had a pregnancy filled with sickness and a premature labor, my husband had lost his job, and we had to move out of our house because of flooding due to burst pipes. The amazing thing is God resolved every single one of these issues before I had any idea that I was sick. We moved into a beautiful new home, we had a healthy little girl, and my husband had a job he loved. For the first time in a long while, I felt like everything was good and I could finally relax. Then cancer hit.

This was the biggest test of my faith yet. I was confused and felt hurt by the God I loved so much. As strange as this sounds, I felt personally attacked by Him. For days, I lay in my hospital bed crying, worrying, and anxiety ridden. I didn't even have a diagnosis yet because I was waiting for my surgery, but the doctors were confident they knew what was going on. In preparing for my surgery, I was terrified. The doctors were concerned because I had a large blood clot in my neck and when you are placed "under" for surgery, clots can move and cause strokes. There was a real chance I would suffer a stroke before I even woke up from surgery. I felt betrayed by God. He knew I was hurting and that I was struggling, but He also knew I was listening more closely than ever before. It was in this moment of darkness and despair God spoke to my heart. As I was being wheeled out of my hospital room, I turned to my family as this intense peace and calm took over me and I just knew everything was going to be fine. I knew I was going to come out of that surgery without suffering a stroke. The Holy Spirit spoke to me that day in a way that I had never experienced.

I share these personal events of my life to encourage you to put your faith in the Lord. Bad things are always going to happen, but you do not have to walk through these times on your own. Look back on your life: in what ways did God prepare you for your battle with cancer? Pray and ask for clarity and for help—He will answer.

"Be strong and courageous, and do the work. Do not be afraid or discouraged, for the Lord God, my God, is with you. He will not fail or forsake you" (1 Chronicles 28:20).

My hope for you is that you will find solace in the stories and feelings I share. I hope you won't feel so alone. Most importantly, I pray you renew or create a relationship with the Lord—that you may find rest in His love and peace in His gospel.

A Letter on
Nothingness

*"The Lord is my shepherd, I lack
nothing."*

Psalm 23:1

Although I just spent a considerable
amount of time discussing my faith,
it's so important for you to know that I
am weak and I do fall short. In fact very
often, I feel nothing. I find myself staring
absentmindedly at the television or a book
literally feeling nothing. I find myself in a
conversation with my mom listening to her

but not feeling anything. This is the scariest emotion of all to me because, in these moments, it seems I have disappeared and when I come back to myself, I am hit with the full weight of my circumstance. And the full weight of my situation is too much to handle. In the letters I received, this was not an emotion that was written on because I don't believe anyone but a person going through a fight with cancer or another illness could understand what it means. The letters I received were always uplifting and positive, which is so important to mental health but sometimes that just wasn't what I needed. Sometimes, I long for someone who gets it when I say I feel nothing—I'm empty. I need someone who not only gets it but also says it's normal to feel this way.

One of the emptiest moments was over something that probably sounds trivial to most people. My sister's wedding was fast approaching. I previously mentioned I come from an ethnic family which means our family events are a big deal. My family is Lebanese but if you have seen the movie, *My Big Fat Greek Wedding,* then you have insight into how my family operates. So, the whole family was at my house talking about my sister's upcoming wedding. I have looked forward to both my sister's weddings my entire life because my older sister, Jess, is my soulmate and my baby sister, Ally, is my best friend. My sisters and mom were picking hairstyles. But I didn't have hair. They talked about their need to keep losing weight so their dresses would look incredible—more incredible than they already do. I gained more than 20 pounds from the steroids in my chemo treatment. I was worried the dress I ordered wouldn't be big enough. They were thrilled at the thought of getting to the reception to eat and dance. I had to bring my own fork, plate, and cup to the reception and the mere thought of dancing made my body tired. I sat there feeling nothing. It was like I did not exist.

I felt like I didn't matter. It was like there was this movie going on in front of me constantly and I was just a faceless member of the audience. I was just a bystander in my own life. Maybe you have these moments. If you do, let me be the one who tells you if you feel yourself feeling nothing, like your existence isn't real anymore, it will pass and it's okay. You may feel like you have vanished and you don't matter, but you are ever so present and you matter so much. Don't allow yourself to crawl deeper into yourself and hide from the world. It's certainly the easy answer but please, don't let yourself do it. Each time you allow yourself to fall into your nothingness, it gets increasingly difficult to come back.

Find someone in your life whom you trust to be your go-to person. A person who will always answer your call and help you out of the dark place that you are in. Someone who will reassure you that you matter and you to keep pushing forward. It's in these moments when you recognize your worth, that cancer doesn't get to win— you do. Always remember that even though you may feel nothing, you are everything to your Father in heaven and you were created in His image and likeness. *"So God created mankind in his own image, in the image of God" (Genesis 1:27).*

A Letter on
Thankfulness

*"Let the peace of Christ rule in
your hearts, since as members of
one body you were called to peace.
And be thankful"*

COLOSSIANS 3:13

Thankfulness during a time of extreme
fear and confusion seems out of place
but it could not be more relevant. Force
yourself to be thankful. It will pull you out
of the valley of darkness that you're in and
bring you to a place of light. Thankfulness

may not seem like the obvious follow up to a letter on nothingness but it's the perfect pair. When you come back from feeling nothing, be thankful. I said nothing was the scariest emotion for me because I'm hit with the weight of my reality, but how I conquer that fear is with thankfulness. Thankfulness to God and thankfulness to those around me. When I was going through treatment, my mom taught me a trick to finding that peacefulness and thankfulness. One morning, around 5:00 AM, I called my mom and through sobs of fear I told her I had the dream again. The one where they walk into the hospital room and tell me it's cancer. Except this is not just a dream, it's my reality. My mom said she would be right over and I heard the click of her phone. Soon, she was walking through my front door carrying a bag. It contained two notebooks and some pens. She told me to open the notebook and start listing off everything I was thankful for and she would do the same in her notebook. Then we shared our lists and we kept going until I felt happiness again. We did this for what seemed like hours.

Try this yourself! Try listing everything you are thankful for and keep listing until you are filled with happiness. I've learned to become thankful for the smallest things. When I was in the hospital, I missed being able to change my daughter's diaper. Now, every mess I get to clean up and every diaper I get to change I'm so thankful. Isn't that what life is anyways? One giant but fun mess we all get to be part of?

In truth, I was never one who believed in the power of the positive and thankful mind. I am a Christian woman who believes strongly in the power of prayer and all that empower your mind stuff seemed silly to me. Now, however, I have realized that forcing yourself to have a positive mindset makes a real difference. I'm not sure what it means medically but mentally it keeps you laughing and smiling and most importantly, strong. My dad was the one who helped me to understand this. He would call me every single day just to make sure my mind was in a good place. If he sensed despair, he would show up at my house to help me find happiness. His concern for me during this time of my life reminded me of how concerned he was for me when I was in labor with my daughter, Cecelia. When he came in the room to meet his first grandchild, he passed the crib and came straight to me. He wanted to thank me for my strength in delivering his first grandchild. Cling to people like this during your times of sorrow and be thankful for them.

If you feel filled with hate or anger and confusion, make your thankful list. It will help fill you with happiness. No one needs to read your list. It can have anything you want on it. Coffee makes it on my list every single time. You can keep one list and reread it or make a new one every time— completely your call. But no matter what, find a way to be thankful.

A LETTER ON FEAR

*"Even though I walk through the
darkest valley, I will fear no evil,
for you are with me; your rod and
staff, they comfort me."*

PSALM 23:4

Take a deep breath. Let it out. Please
know fear is the most natural feeling
in the world for a cancer patient. Fear of the
unknown. Fear of the lack of control. Fear
of the treatments and tests. I have moments
where I am absolutely terrified. It comes
from this place deep inside me and I feel it

in my gut. I look at my daughter and fear takes over me. It's not fear about not living my life but fear that she might live hers without me. I look at my mom and I register heartbreak in her eyes and I become scared. I know what she's thinking: *Why my child? Why can't I switch places with her? What did I do wrong?*

I firmly believe I didn't know true fear until I was given my diagnosis. I'll never forget the doctor saying, "Jennifer, it's just as we thought—lymphoma." I felt my face turn white. My stomach turned and turned. I couldn't hear anything anymore. I had so many questions but nothing was making its way from my brain to my mouth. My mom was crying and talking to the doctor. She was asking the questions that I should have been asking. My best friend, Kayla, walked in the room and I imagine my mom gave her the news because I saw terror take over her face. Fear continued to consume me—I still couldn't hear. I wasn't even sure I was crying. I know my insides were crying—sobbing actually—but my face felt stone-cold. I was face-to-face with fear. It was intimate. It was terrifying. It was true fear.

It's a year post-chemo. I am deemed "cancer free" and being closely monitored. But I wake up every single day with the fear that the cancer will come back. I question every decision I make and I call my oncologist over something as simple as a sneeze. It brings back that fear of the unknown. I don't know how I got cancer, so I'm always worried that something I'm doing is going to bring it back. It doesn't matter how many times my oncology team tells me my prognosis is great, I worry and I'm scared. I have so much left I want to do and experience so I am constantly trying to push fast-forward on my life instead of being present in the moment.

There are so many times in my life now where I wish I could go back to having the fear of a child. Can you remember the things you were once scared of? Spiders? A dark room at night? Monsters under your bed? Going into the basement by yourself? I want so badly to be fearful of a spider or a dark room at night, but I have to remind myself I'm not a child anymore. *"When I was a child, I talked like a child, I thought like a child, I reasoned like a child. When I became a man, I put the ways of childhood behind me"* (1 Corinthians 13:11). As an adult, I can look back on my childhood fears and recognize the silliness. I'm hoping that twenty years from now, I will look back on my experience with cancer in the same way I reflect upon my childhood. If nothing else, I want to be stronger and not so afraid. Then my mind wanders—shouldn't twenty or thirty years from now be the time when I first experience a life-threatening illness? Why did I have to go through this so young? Does wisdom come with age or experience?

When I was in high school I was senior class president, and therefore had to give a speech AT graduation. The theme of my speech was "There is a time for everything."

This was taken directly from my current gospel reading at the time. *"There is a time for everything, and a season for every activity under the heavens: a time to be born and a time to die, a time to plant and a time to uproot, a time to kill and a time to heal, a time to tear down and a time to build up, a time to weep and a time to laugh, a time to mourn and a time to dance, a time to scatter stones and a time to gather them, a time to embrace and a time to refrain, a time to search and a time to give up, a time to keep and a time to throw away, a time to tear and a time to mend, a time to be silent and a time to speak, a time to love and a time to hate, a time for war and a time for peace"* *(Ecclesiastes 3:1-8).* The irony of my own speech! Was I preparing myself for the time of cancer? As I reflect upon my speech and the verses I took it from, I am realizing that for each time there is a heartache, it is followed by a time of relief. So I guess there is a time for cancer and a time to be cancer-free. I want to stop living my life in fear that I still have cancer. I need to take the advice of my eighteen-year-old self and the words of the gospel and allow myself to rest in the belief that this is my time to be cancer free.

If I let it, fear could control every part of my life. But what good would that do? None at all. Maybe you're feeling fear right now. While it's normal, you do not have to let it overtake you. It does not need to have a hold on you. Push yourself to move past it. How? Pray. Make your thankful list. Call your go-to person. Most importantly, pray. Ask God to ease your suffering and help you through your pain. You have more control than you think in this situation. You can't control your diagnosis, side effects, or outcome but you can control your perspective and your mindfulness. I'm not perfect and while I sit here giving advice, I have a difficult time taking my own advice. Fear regularly takes over me. But we have to try to overcome it, don't we? We owe ourselves that much.

A Letter on
Perspective

"For our light and momentary troubles are achieving for us an eternal glory that far outweighs them all. So we fix our eyes not on what is seen, but what is unseen, since what is seen is temporary, but what is unseen is eternal."

2 Corinthians 4:17–18

I remember the exact moment I changed my perspective on my cancer and, as result, I became incredibly empowered.

My mom and I were at the wig shop. I still had my hair but the doctors warned me it would start falling out soon. I was scared and felt I had lost all control over every aspect of my life. But sitting in the chair with a wig on my head, I decided I would be the one to say when and how I lost my hair. I stopped viewing it as something that was just happening to me and started seeing it as something I could embrace as a sign of healing. So, I took my time trying on every wig I could until I found "the one" that made me feel most like myself. I made a promise to myself that I would not watch myself deteriorate but rather, I would shave my head at the first sign of hair loss.

It was two weeks after my first chemo treatment when I pulled the first chunk of hair out. My initial instinct was to cry my eyes out—which I did. Then I remembered the promise I made to myself. Pulling one chunk of hair out was already enough for me. I couldn't watch myself slowly fall apart. So I called my hairstylist cousin, Dana, and asked her to come over and shave my head that night. After I reached out to her, I called a bunch of my family members and asked them if they would come support me that night. Every single person I called was there and together, we took control of one tiny aspect of my cancer.

By changing my perspective—my outlook—on cancer's control of my life, I was able to have this intense moment of empowerment. It was my choice to take that step. You are probably thinking of ways you have already done this or maybe ways in which you could—I encourage you to grab hold of these things and instead of wallowing and feeling defeated, take the reins! Turn something awful into something good! It will change your life and unleash confidence you didn't know you had inside you.

Because of this, the next time I was presented with the opportunity to change my perspective, I excitedly took it! Since I'm a teacher, there was no way I could be around my students while undergoing such intense chemo. So, I had to take the year off. I was heartbroken. I love my students—my job was a dream come true for me. I spent so much time crying and feeling sorry for myself until one day I realized this was a blessing. I came to understand that my year off was a gift from God because He was giving me an abundance of the one thing I was most concerned about—having time with my daughter. From that moment, I stopped feeling like something was taken from me and instead realized I was given the best present of all.

I can't thank God enough that He allowed me to have that time with Cece. We made so many special memories and grew closer than ever. Most of all, I've realized the truth of the verse above. These things are temporary and when we stop fixating our gaze on them, we see the bigger picture. My hair came back. The wig was donated. I went back to work. Unlimited time with Cece was gone in the blink of an eye. I'm glad I was able to embrace these moments as part of the healing process. What things are you suffering from right now that you can turn into positives? Can you be strong enough to view nausea as healing? Can you view the loss of feeling in your hands and feet as a sign that the medicine is working? And can you view your bald head as a sign that your body is responding the way you need it to? Most importantly, pray and ask God to help you find ways to shift your focus and your outlook. Keep going, my friend—you can do this!

A LETTER ON LOVE

"Dear friends, let us love one another, for love comes from God. Everyone who loves has been born of God and knows God. Whoever does not love does not know God, because God is love...There is no fear in love. But perfect love drives out fear."

1 JOHN 4:7–8, 18

I stumbled upon true love the day I met my husband. We were just nineteen years old and trying to have fun in college while also passing our classes. I knew I loved him differently from any other guy I had ever met. I viewed him as a man. A man who is intelligent and loves the Lord. A man who had a real plan for his life. He is sweet, kind, and he shows empathy. Not to mention, he is fearfully handsome. I wanted to be his person. To my delight, he wanted to be my person too. The day he asked me to be his girlfriend, my mom asked me how I felt knowing I just had my last first kiss.

As a nineteen-year-old girl, I thought I knew Larry. I could easily rattle off a list of reasons for why I loved him. It wasn't until the day our daughter was born that I learned a little more about him. He never left my side throughout the 10 hours I was in labor. When our Cecelia was born, the first thing he did was throw his arms around me and tell me I was his hero. He cried as he held me and in that moment, I found out more about the depth of his appreciation and respect for me. I discovered his integrity and intense loyalty the day I ended up in the hospital. And I fell even more in love. I feel silly when I question his devotion to me because he has never once wavered. He is steadfast and strong. He picks up where I fall short. Since the day I was diagnosed, he has been at my side asking the doctors questions, researching lymphoma, and doing everything he possibly can to ensure I receive the best care. He has put his life on hold to make sure mine keeps going—that, to me, is true love. Larry is the love of my life, but this experience has taught me that I barely know my husband. I look forward to spending the rest of my life discovering more about his heart and soul.

I would have never expected cancer to teach me about love. It has shown me the pure goodness in those around me. Not only have I fallen deeper in love with my husband, but also the unconditional love I have for my daughter has strengthened. My love for her was immediate. The day I heard her heartbeat from inside my body, I knew I was in trouble! My whole body just melted and I knew I would love that little baby for my entire life. When she was born, I was breathless. It was as if I gave everything I had, even the very breath from my body, to her. I have spent my life devoting myself to her and her well-being. But two weeks after my first chemo treatment, my sweet two-year-old displayed her unconditional love for me. I had just lost all of my hair and I was scared that she would be afraid of me. I was lying on the couch feeling insecure and nervous as my mom went to get Cece out of her bed. I saw her walking out of her room and I immediately put a hat on. She came teetering into the living room and started crying when she saw me. She kept saying, "Mommy, take off your hat." So I did what any good parent does and I listened to my two-year-old. I took off my hat and she came running into my arms. Then she did the most magical thing I have ever experienced: she sat next to me on the couch, pulled me into her lap, and began rubbing my bald head. I was a grown

woman who was lying in her child's lap crying her eyes out. God knew I needed my
daughter's acceptance and He gave it to me
in a way that broke me down and then made
me incredibly brave. Through Cece, God
taught me that any person at any point in
their life can show unconditional love.

These momentous moments continued throughout my chemo treatment. After
diagnosis, my mom basically moved into
my house to take care of me and Cece so
Larry could continue going to work. Once I
had completed a chemo treatment, I would
be down for about ten days. Sick, nauseous,
and even too tired to walk, but my mom
was always there. Her strength for me was
remarkable. After my second treatment,
my mom came down with a cold. It broke
her heart that she couldn't be around me.
It was during this time that she showed the
depth of a mother's love. One afternoon I
woke up from a nap, sat up in my bed, and
saw my mom sitting outside my bedroom
window. She had brought a chair outside

and had been sitting there my entire nap, making sure she could still keep a close eye on me. I don't think my parents ever left my side during my entire battle. They taught me that being a parent means feeling the intensity of your child's pain but also being the reason they can persevere. Once again, I found myself learning so much more about people in my life that I thought I had already figured out.

I constantly wish that I could have learned these things about my parents, husband, and daughter in a different way. Regardless, I am so grateful for the opportunity to know them more. I hope that you can find a deeper way to love as you embark on your journey with cancer. I pray there are people around you who are showing their true, beautiful colors, and you are embracing it. Finding the good in your life right now has to be something you do because if not, then you will fall into despair. Find the good. Find the love.

A Letter on
Brokenness

"The Lord is close to the broken-hearted and saves those who are crushed in spirit."

PSALM 34:18

When we think of something that's broken, we often think about items we use that no longer work and need fixing or replacing. Most of the time, it's our own fault something is broken. We easily accept responsibility—albeit annoyed with ourselves—but we do what it takes to resolve the issue. But what do you do when your spirit and identity are crushed to pieces, yet you did nothing to cause it?

If you feel broken, you are not alone. Cancer does break you. It takes you apart piece by piece until you don't recognize yourself anymore. It tears your life into shreds and challenges everything you thought you knew about yourself. But when you finally get the energy to pick yourself up, you end up learning new things about yourself. You're stronger than you thought. You can love deeper than you knew. And your cancer is only one tiny piece of who you are as a person. This realization, however, does not come naturally or easily.

I remember sitting at the head table at my sister's wedding reception. My wig was styled beautifully and my makeup perfect. My bridesmaid dress ended up fitting and I even remembered to pack comfortable shoes. There was a line of people waiting to talk to me all night and to each one of them, I looked just as I should. I looked completely put together. I assured them all that I was doing fine—that my spirits were good and I was happy as can be. But I wasn't fine. I was surrounded by everything I no longer was. I looked down at my sister embarking on her new married life. I looked down the table to my husband and wondered if he regretted marrying me now. My heart cracked a little. I listened to my cousin tell me about her new opportunities at work and I was reminded that my work had to give my job away. My heart cracked a little more. I looked around the room and saw my pregnant cousins. I looked down at my stomach thinking I might never have another baby. My heart shattered. I was completely broken. I made my apologies and left the wedding early. It was all just too much.

I found out the hard way that my identity was resting on a fluid foundation and not on the Lord. The only true way to heal my identity and find worth in myself again was to rely completely on Jesus. The way my identity was stripped to nothing reminded me that true beauty is not external but internal. I think this is something we say we understand and know but it isn't until we are presented a tough situation that we really get it. Each stage of cancer has broken a piece of me and I have had to teach myself to rediscover my inner beauty and my worth. It seems like a silly thing, but losing my hair was one of the toughest parts—aside from the chemo. As a woman, you spend so much time crafting your outward appearance and to have that taken from you in an instant is earth-shattering. I spent a considerable amount of my life teaching myself to style my hair perfectly. I dedicated myself to losing weight and exercising. I felt beautiful and I was proud of the work I had done. Then I gained more weight from the chemo than I did when I was pregnant, and my hair was gone within fourteen days of my first chemo treatment. I found myself angry with God again but instead of remaining angry, I started to pray and listen closely. I was once again having one of those intimate moments where my faith was getting ready to grow. I was lying in bed one night and this verse just kept swimming around in my head. I had heard it so many times but I was understanding it differently: *"Charm is deceptive, and beauty is fleeting; but a woman who fears the Lord is to be praised," (Proverbs 31:30).* I realized that in the barrenness of my appearance, I needed to redirect myself to the Lord and pay attention to the good He is doing in my life. Even though I was taught this verse all my life, it somehow helped me to change perspective. I no longer cared about my bald head. I wanted my beauty and purpose to come from a place of being a strong Christian woman who loved the Lord, and I no longer desired to be obsessed with the material expectations of the world.

Allow yourself to accept your beauty in your new life. Listen close to what God may be trying to teach you in these moments, and remember that true grace and beauty stems from loving the Lord.

A LETTER ON
STRENGTH

"Three times I pleaded with the Lord to take it away from me. But He said to me, 'My grace is sufficient for you, for my power is made perfect in weakness.' Therefore I will boast all the more gladly about my weaknesses, so that Christ's power may rest on me. That is why, I delight in weaknesses, in insults, in hardships, in persecutions, in difficulties. For when I am weak, then I am strong."

2 CORINTHIANS 12:8–10

Stop. Go back and reread that passage. What is Jesus telling us? He is telling us, explicitly, that we will be weak but it will be all for His glory. This passage is so humbling and convicting. We are reminded that we are not the most important thing in this world. We are reminded that we are here to bring light to His kingdom and His power. Let that sink in because if you do, you will realize that your struggle is not in vain. God is using your battle and struggle for bigger and better things—for Him! Don't let this make you angry, but rather embrace it and allow yourself to be weak because in that, you will find strength.

My strength was tested that day of my second biopsy surgery. I had been on the surgery recovery floor for about 24 hours. They had to cut into my chest to get to the tumor for the biopsy. The surgery was very invasive and painful. They even had to remove part of my rib bone. After the surgery, they gave me this clicker and when I was feeling pain, I was supposed to click the button. It worked really well. So well, it would make my body incredibly comfortable and I would fall into a deep sleep. I even asked my mom to hit my button every 6 minutes when I was sleeping to make sure I stayed asleep. When they moved me back to the oncology floor, they wanted to take my clicker away. I about lost it. For the last 24 hours, I had hit that button every 6 minutes. It calmed my mind. It let me fall into deep, restful sleeps. I did not think I was strong enough to have it taken away. I was afraid that I couldn't handle the pain of the surgery site and the chest tube site. It didn't matter what I wanted. The nurse came in and let me click the button one more time, then she took it away. I crumbled and felt that I had reached the weakest point in my life. Then my husband began to pray with me. We prayed and cried and prayed some more but when we were done, I knew I could do it. When asked why, my answer was simple: I placed all my pain and fears on Jesus, and He was carrying me through this. It was a painful and physical test of the strength of my faith, but pushing through demonstrated that even at my weakest, God made me strong. God was the only way, and His power and glory was shown that day—not mine.

I still get pain in the surgery sites. The doctor said I probably will for most of my life. At this point, the pain I get is manageable and it passes quickly. Physically, I feel stronger with each passing day but mentally, I still haven't healed from that surgery and I need to remind myself daily to cast my pain on Him. Every single time I look in a mirror and see the gash on the left side of my chest, I have to fight back tears because it's a visual and constant reminder that I am weak.

Finding strength is a daily obstacle. Once again I sit here preaching to you, but please know this is one of those areas where I struggle to take my own advice. I became familiar with all of the physical struggles that cancer and chemotherapy brought upon my body: the nausea, the fatigue, the flulike symptoms, the neuropathy, and the general discomfort. It's the mental obstacles that take their toll. The way in which I think things through is different. I ask myself hundreds of questions a day about every little thing. If I look to the future too much, I get nervous. If I spend time away from my daughter, I stress and become frantic until she is back in my arms. These are the side effects of cancer and chemotherapy that the doctors don't seem to address. It's in these times that I need the Lord but struggle to lean on Him.

If you find yourself feeling weak, then rest easy knowing there is at least one other person in this world feeling the exact same thing. We don't have to be weak. When I feel myself losing my drive and my strength, I take a bunch of deep breaths and focus as hard as I can on one thing I need to overcome. I don't always overcome it right away. Sometimes I dump everything I am feeling onto my husband or my mom. I try to pray and give it to God. But most of the time I sit up alone at night and cry until I have nothing left. I cry until I'm so tired from crying, I crash back into my pillow. When will I be normal again? When will I feel like myself again?

I am trying to find peace in the unknown in my life and through that, I am hoping to find strength. I do not have all of the answers for you. I don't even have them for myself. But I want you to know you're strong and you have it inside of you to persevere. Keep moving forward, my friend. We can do this.

A Letter on
Confidence

*"For you have been my hope,
Sovereign Lord, my confidence
since my youth."*

PSALM 71:5

I remember the first time I went to the grocery store after my diagnosis. It had taken me months to gain the confidence to walk into a public place. I was filled with fear but mainly I was insecure. Before my diagnosis, I spent zero part of my life feeling insecure. I was confident in myself and my abilities. I knew who I wanted to be and I tried to make decisions that would turn me into that person. But there I sat in my Jeep outside of Randazzo Marketplace. I was wearing a mask and latex gloves. I had my hat pulled so low you could barely see my eyebrows. I had a package of disinfecting wipes ready to wipe down the grocery cart. My hand was on the door handle but I just couldn't seem to pull it. My head was flooded with questions. What will people think? Will they stare? Will they give me that same look of pity I know too well? Will they cough or sneeze near me? How will I know if I caught something? My phone buzzed, interrupting my thoughts. It was my mom wondering what was taking me so long. She needed the roast I was supposed to be getting so she could put it in the crock pot. I took a deep breath, pulled the handle, and got out of the car. I grabbed the cart next to me and began scrubbing it down. A woman started walking over to me. She had a young child with her. I started to get nervous. I wanted to jump into my car. Instead, she called out to me. "How are you feeling?" she asked me. Do I know this woman? Now I was the one staring as I tried to figure out who she was. She continued, "How many treatments do you still have?" I responded, "Just one more." She continued questioning me. She wanted to know if she could walk through the store with me and help me. See, she had lymphoma and knew exactly how it felt to be me. I thanked her for her time but told her I was fine by myself. Tears welled up in my eyes and I took a moment to thank God for sending her to restore my confidence. I believe with my whole heart God placed that woman there to help me. She was like an angel sent to encourage me to keep living and keep going.

To think I was afraid to go into a store might seem odd to most people. But you probably know exactly what I'm talking about and how I felt. It was liberating to have that woman treat me with such kindness and love—a true angel on Earth. If you're feeling insecure and lacking confidence, just know there are good people in the world who want you to feel included and safe. Don't question yourself. Get out and live your life. It will help you get back to the person you want to be.

A LETTER ON
LONELINESS

"Jesus answered, It is written: Man shall not live on bread alone, but on every word that comes from the mouth of God."

MATTHEW 4:4

M y daughter came to visit me at the hospital for the first time. I had been there for five days of what would be a two-week stay—the longest she and I had ever been apart. She kept asking everyone for me so my husband and I decided it's best she came to see me. She sat in bed with me and we played and read books. Larry brought the stroller so I walked her through the hospital while he pushed my IV. She stayed for about an hour because it was nearing bedtime and she needed a bath. A bath I couldn't give her and bedtime songs I couldn't sing. I kissed her and held her, then sent her home with Larry. As I watched them walk out of my hospital room to go home to live life without me, I broke down. This time there were no tears. There was no panicked cry. I couldn't talk or even look at anyone. I wanted to run out of the room with them, but my IV would have stopped me. The mass in my chest would have made me short of breath. I was a prisoner of the cancer. There was nothing inside me except complete and utter loneliness.

I struggle to take my own advice. I told you I feel alone on a regular basis and I mean that. But as time passes and I learn to love and accept myself again, the moments of loneliness become less frequent. I realized

I can't rely on others to make me feel validated in what I am feeling, and I can't rely on others to keep me from feeling lonely. The reason being: no one is going through what I am going through. As much as your family and friends try to keep you feeling surrounded with love, the only person who needs to show you love is you! You have to accept this hand you were dealt and defeat your natural instinct to feel alone. The only way I have been able to overcome this is by finding purpose and companionship with Jesus. He knows my struggles better than I do. He knows what I am going to feel long before I feel it. I have learned to love myself and find comfort in solitude solely because of the relationship I have with Him.

The day Cece came to visit me still burns a hole in my heart, but I have grown since then. I force myself to think positively and not let that hurt take over my heart. I pray and I find myself in conversation with the Lord regularly. I now completely understand what it means when God says we will live on His words and His gospel. Feeling alone is a real side effect of a cancer diagnosis but it's treatable. Allow yourself to focus on the positive and through that, peace in your heart.

A LETTER ON LIFE

"No one can come to me unless the Father who sent me draws them, and I will raise them up at the last day...Very truly I tell you, the one who believes has eternal life. I am the bread of life."

JOHN 6:44–48

I started writing this at twenty-eight and now I just celebrated my thirtieth birthday. When I look back on these last thirty years, I realize the most important thing I have learned so far is to trust the Lord. Trust

Him with your life. Give it all to Him and do not hold anything back. I am so grateful I made the decision all those years ago to to accept the Lord as my Savior. Since then, I have lived my life walking with Him. It's true I have encountered the most difficult times in the last few years, but I have never felt more alive. I have never been more sure of who I am and how I want to live the rest of my years on earth. Until recently, I used to tell people that when I come face-to-face with Jesus, the first thing I plan on asking Him is "Why did you give me cancer?" I would, however, like to change that and instead I want to hug Him and say "THANK YOU"—for in that struggle He taught me what it means to truly live.

My final wish for you is that you will close this book and feel empowered in your weakness. Go in faith and live your life!

CPSIA information can be obtained
at www.ICGtesting.com
Printed in the USA
BVHW04061509022
628472BV00005B/12

9 781595 557247